W9-BWV-192

ERIC P. UPHILL

EGYPTIAN TOWNS AND CITIES

SHIRE EGYPTOLOGY

Cover illustration
Deir el-Medina village.
(Photograph by Eric P. Uphill.)

British Library Cataloguing in Publication Data available.

Published by
SHIRE PUBLICATIONS LTD
Cromwell House, Church Street, Princes Risborough,
Aylesbury, Bucks HP17 9AJ, UK

Series Editor: Barbara Adams

Copyright © Eric P. Uphill, 1988.
All rights reserved.
No part of this publication may be reproduced or transmitted
in any form or by any means, electronic or mechanical,
including photocopy, recording, or any information storage
and retrieval system, without permission in writing
from the publishers.

ISBN 0 85263 939 2

First published 1988

Set in 11 point Times and printed in Great Britain by
C. I. Thomas & Sons (Haverfordwest) Ltd,
Press Buildings, Merlins Bridge, Haverfordwest, Dyfed.

Contents

Acknowledgements

In writing this study on urban development I owe a debt to a number of people. In the first place to Mrs Barbara Adams, Editor of the Shire Egyptology series, for her help in the actual production of the book. Likewise to those artists who have made the plans and drawings, John Kirby for figure 2 and Helena Jaeschke of Archaeoptyx (Archaeological Drawing Services) for the remainder. Lastly to my wife for typing the manuscript and for constant help in preparing it for publication. All photographs used as illustrations are my own, taken during many trips to Egypt, and are intended to show a selection of the many urban sites known, particularly those mentioned in the text.

4

List of illustrations

Chronology

After Murnane, W. J., *The Penguin Guide to Ancient Egypt*, 1983.

Palaeolithic	500,000 - 5500 BC	500,000 BC Lower Palaeolithic 100,000 BC Middle Palaeolithic 30,000 BC Upper Palaeolithic 10,000 - 5500 BC Epi-Palaeolithic

Predynastic	5500 - 3050 BC		
		5500 - 4000 BC	
		Lower Egypt	Fayum A, Merimda
		Upper Egypt	Badarian
		4000 - 3500 BC	
		Lower Egypt	?Omari A,
		Upper Egypt	Amratian (Naqada I)
		3500 - 3300 BC	
		Lower Egypt	?Omari B
		Upper Egypt	Early Gerzean (Naqada II)
		3500 - 3050 BC	
		Lower Egypt	Maadi
		3300 - 3150 BC	
		Upper Egypt	Late Gerzean (Naqada II)

Protodynastic	3200 - 3050 BC	Naqada III (Late Gerzean)
Early Dynastic	3050 - 2613 BC	Dynasties I - II
Old Kingdom	2613 - 2181 BC	Dynasties III - VI
First Intermediate Period	2181 - 2040 BC	Dynasties VII - XI (1)
Middle Kingdom	2040 - 1782 BC	Dynasties XI (2) - XII
Second Intermediate Period	1782 - 1570 BC	Dynasties XIII - XVII
New Kingdom	1570 - 1070 BC	Dynasties XVIII - XX
Third Intermediate Period	1070 - 713 BC	Dynasties XXI - XXIV
Late Period	713 - 332 BC	Dynasties XXV - XXXI
Graeco-Roman Period	332 BC - AD 395	Ptolemies and Roman Emperors

1
Introduction

Egyptian hieroglyphs use two terms for an urban growth: *niwt,* meaning a city, and *dmi,* a town or settlement. The former appears to denote a natural growth, whether large or small, the latter a planned one.

The dwellings which composed these were called *pr,* which means house in the general sense as well as the specific building for occupation, and *hwt,* which covers the yard or walled enclosure as well as the house proper. Both terms were used for town houses and country villas.

Geographically Egypt falls into two parts, the delta in the north and the Nile valley in the centre and south, that is, Lower and Upper Egypt. Throughout the historical period most of Egypt was bare, arid desert with a few oases providing the only places to support any life. Out of a total area of 386,000 square miles (1,000,000 sq km) less than 13,500 square miles (35,000 sq km) were cultivable as recently as 1947, a figure that probably exceeds that in Pharaonic times.

The earliest Egyptian dwellings appear to have been simple reed huts or even wind-breaks rather than caves as in palaeolithic Europe. Tiny groups of these, too small even to be termed villages, would have been found on the sparsely vegetated lands bordering the Nile valley and the delta, and possibly on the sand-spits which rose like islands throughout the uncultivated and untamed districts which were later to form the centres of the urban population of the Two Kingdoms.

As the earliest Egyptians progressed in the art of building many materials were at hand. Various kinds of wood were available as well as reeds, rushes, papyrus and palm ribs. Two kinds of planks could be made from two species of palm tree, the date and the dom. Acacia *(nilotica)* and tamarisk were other local woods useful for house building. Only later, when very large beams were needed for roofing palaces or making columns and temple flagstaffs, were cedar and other imported woods used extensively. Palm fronds, with open and closed bud, and papyrus influenced the design of column and capital.

Mud, and later mud-brick, formed the second great class of building material. Bricks (ancient Egyptian *dbt,* Coptic *TWWBE,* Arabic *adobi*) were easily made once the technique of strengthening lumps of river clay had been evolved. They were at first used with, and later instead of, the simple wattle and daub of earlier Predynastic times.

Brickmaking was a highly involved art which had to be learnt over a long period and used wooden moulds of very varied sizes. The best bricks were mixed with chopped straw, but quite a useful brick could be made by using sand instead. Normally they were simply dried in the sun, although baked clay tiles were used for special functions. Mortar was merely mud of similar constituency to the bricks.

Stone formed the third main class of building material for houses and domestic buildings and later temples and tombs were built entirely in stone. In houses and palaces it was mainly reserved for column bases and sometimes door-cases and window grilles in the better built mansion houses, but even here it was used sparingly. Wooden column shaft bases could suffer damage from wet rot or insects, and stone bases acted as a protection and were much wider than the wooden shafts.

Although they had certain drawbacks and limitations Egyptian houses were in general well built and planned from at least Early Dynastic times, and perfectly adapted to suit the particular climate of the region in which they were erected. Few other civilisations, except perhaps that of the ancient Indus valley, can have equalled them, nor do they seem to have been improved on until Hellenistic and Roman times.

Throughout the following chapters estimates of population are calculated on a maximum total of 250 people an acre (0.4 ha). This ratio is based on findings at Deir el-Medina, where on 1½ acres (0.6 ha) a figure of 350 was obtained (nearly 240 per acre), and at Amarna, where the figure was up to about 370 per acre or 1½ times the figure used.

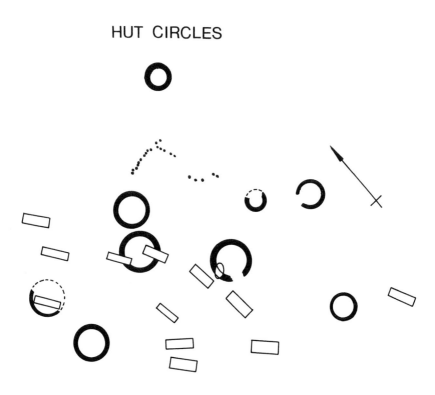

1. Hemamiya. Plan of a Naqada I village. (Drawing by Helena Jaeschke.)

2
Natural urban growth: prehistoric background

As the first Egyptian settlements appear to have been composed of flimsy reed shelters of which little or no traces remain, there is not much that can be said about villages or dwellings in Egypt until the advent of the neolithic culture around 6000-5500 BC. In order to deal effectively with an ever increasing amount of material after this date the sites are divided into three periods, set within the framework of Upper and Lower Egypt to allow for regional differences.

In Upper Egypt the earliest type sites are those associated with the culture known by the modern Arabic place name of Badari. Before 5000 BC cemeteries had been separated from the villages where, as at Matmar, five small settlements or hamlets made up a larger community situated on small rock spurs at the edge of the valley. While little remained of the huts, some granaries were found. These consisted of circular pits sunk into the ground, a typical one measuring 8 feet 10 inches (2.7 metres) in diameter and 9 feet 10 inches (3 metres) deep. Such containers were common throughout Egypt during this period, although generally smaller and normally lined with basketry or mud.

At Badari itself several more villages were similarly placed along a stretch of several miles. Once again only the underground storage pits remained, but scattered objects and ashes from fires showed the areas of the actual habitations.

The form of these huts must be inferred, but from examples of slightly later date at other sites they would seem to have been round and of beehive shape, constructed of reeds and mud. Cooking was done before the door as there was no arrangement for dealing with smoke and the fire risk would have been lessened.

From the next period, Naqada I, some actual hut remains at Hemamiya have provided more positive evidence (figure 1). They were dated by associated pottery to approximately just before 3600 BC. Built of wattle and daub, they had internal diameters varying from 7 feet (2.1 metres) to as little as 3 feet (1 metre), with wall thicknesses of 1 foot 2 or 3 inches (37 cm). Their wall heights ranged from 1 foot 6 inches (46 cm) to 2 feet 9 inches (84 cm). Clearly some were not dwellings and one was proved to be a fuel store, the small sizes generally suggesting they were merely peripheral encampments and probably not representative of living conditions in the valley. The mud walls formed little more than a skirting for a thatched superstructure, indicated by the imprint of reed stalks pressed into the moist wall clay. One hut also had a strong untrimmed post of tamarisk wood 14 inches long by 9 inches in circumference (35 by 22.5 cm). As the entrance had to be above the sunken walling the owners had to descend a drop equal to the wall height. No traces of steps were found.

Another stage in the evolution of the Upper Egyptian house is shown at El Mahasna, the hut plans being neither round nor oval but rectangular, corresponding to tombs of approximately 3600 BC. The building technique was the same, posts with interlaced branches and mud-plastered, but the buildings were more substantial. Far more informative, however, is a house excavated at Hierakonpolis in 1979 and dated by associated artefacts to about 3700-3600 BC *(Journal of Near Eastern Studies* 39 [1980], 119-37, where it is termed structure II). It is the first rectangular Predynastic Egyptian house to be systematically excavated. Still semi-subterranean, it measured 13 feet 2 inches long by 11 feet 6 inches wide (4 by 3.5 metres) and consisted of a single room from 1 foot 6 inches to 2 feet 7½ inches deep (45 to 80 cm). It had a superstructure of post, wattle and daub construction, with mud-plastered windscreens of the type today called *zeriba,* attached to the north and east walls. Another innovation was the use of shaped bricks found in the plaster as well as other material. Significantly the excavator, Michael Hoffman, noted the plan's resemblance to the Egyptian hieroglyph *pr,* or 'house'. An oven built on a low platform was found inside.

The development of the Lower Egyptian sites followed a similar pattern but with certain planning differences due to other customs and needs. The Fayum A settlements are of approximately the same age as Badarian, but of a very ephemeral character in that they produced no burials, suggesting these were peripheral settlements inhabited by some migratory people who occupied the edges of the great lake on promontories or *koms.* No house remains were recovered by the excavators, only the hearths and sunken granaries indicating the position of the lightly built huts.

A community which was certainly much better organised and has provided far more evidence of house building and communal planning is Merimda-Beni Salame, excavated before the Second World War. The site is on the south-west desert edge of the delta and proved to have been rebuilt three times before being abandoned after a long period, when it was engulfed in the desert sand. The site covers an area of no less than 660 by 440 yards (600 by 400 metres) or about 44 acres (17.5 ha), a vast spread for a Predynastic settlement. In later levels the huts were built fairly regularly along a street. Revised carbon-14 dating suggests a date of about 4880 BC. The earliest dwellings were again mere shelters of oval plan measuring 10 to 13 feet (3 to 4 metres) in width and opening north-west away from the direction of the prevailing north wind. Holes containing wooden post remains indicated the use of partitions or screens of reeds, a 24 foot 7 inch (7.5 metre) section of one being found buried in the ground. Some of these may have served as workshops or cattle shelters. Other similar huts were ovals of 10 feet 6 inches by 6 feet 6 inches (3.2 by 2 metres) or less and again also served for storage, being similar to those of Mahasna. Walls were built on foundations of debris; sometimes prismatic bricks were found or else large and irregular-shaped mud and chaff-brick blocks. Hut floors were plastered and provided with a sunken vessel to drain off intrusive rain water. Here the dead were buried beneath hut floors, possibly after the dwelling was abandoned, and this custom recalls Mesopotamian practice rather than Nilotic. If the whole site was fully occupied at one time, and it is a debatable point, then the computed population could have been as high as 16,000 people. This, as W. C. Hayes pointed out (1965), would make it one of the largest, if not the largest, prehistoric settlement in Egypt, rivalled only by the later Predynastic town site at Hierakonpolis.

El Omari is a similar type site on the east bank of the Nile south of Cairo, 1¾ miles (3 km) north-east of Helwan. The adjusted carbon-14 date for its first phase is 4570 BC and its duration was long enough to reach the end of the Predynastic period. It spread over a large area and contained two types of dwelling: oval huts with wooden walls resting on stone bases and round ones half dug into the earth and surmounted by a light superstructure. Silos and storage pits cut into the rock were fairly frequent. As at Hierakonpolis a much larger unroofed enclosure or *zeriba* was found which contained the hut and was surrounded by a reed fence stretched on wooden posts. The excavator likened it to the later hieroglyphic determinative for the verb *sbh,* to wall in. The dead were again buried within the village under house floors.

Maadi is the logical successor of El Omari and contemporary with its later phase, that is, about 3600 BC. Like Omari, it was

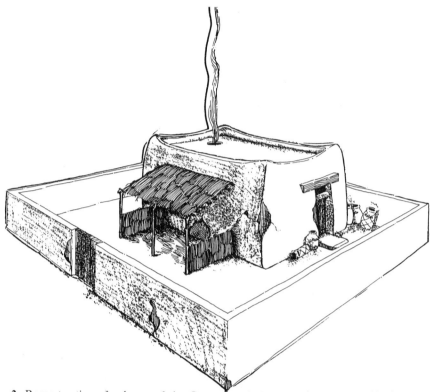

2. Reconstruction of a house of the Gerzean period. (Drawing by John Kirby.)

excavated before 1939. It is late neolithic in type and occupied the south end of a great basin extending from Old Cairo to Tura. The settlement lay on a very narrow low ridge between two wadis and extended roughly east-west. Implements were distributed over an area just under one mile (1.5 km) long by only 393 feet (120 metres) wide, the area covered being around 45 acres (18 ha) in all. Many wooden post ends were found marking the positions of hut walls. These were of tamarisk and from 1½ to 8 inches (4 to 20 cm) thick. Plans were confused, however, because the remains of the huts were at different levels, thus marking different points of occupation. Again, these plans proved to be oval with door openings to the south-west. The entrance was about 14 feet (4.3 metres) wide and the middle of the opening contained a hearth. Clearly the large area of these entrances was not all roofed in, the hut itself taking up only a part. Three layers of buildings need not have meant very long occupation because of the insubstantial nature of the reed and mud walling. Foundations of a square or rectangular house were also found, the wall bases cut into breccia-formed grooves 6 to 8 inches (15 to 20 cm) wide and over 8 feet 3 inches (2.5 metres) long. Horizontal beams must once have been laid in these trenches to form a basic framework. Here again, and for the first time in northern Egypt, is a rectangular house belonging to a class of home measuring about 17 feet long (5.18 metres; 10 cubits?) north to west by 10 feet (3 metres) wide. This house had its door near the south end of the long eastern side. No hearth was found but a cruciform partition existed just inside the doorway, a circular storage (?) pit near the east wall and another rectangular pit outside the entrance. This dwelling has accordingly been compared to the square post-hole houses at Merimda and to a clay model of a Gerzean house in the British Museum (figure 2).

After 3600 BC the two different cultural areas of Egypt began to grow closer together. Known as Naqada II in the south and Gerzean in the north, this final Predynastic era was one of great development and saw the widespread use of metals, stoneworking, the introduction of writing and a vast increase in irrigation and agriculture. As a result the population must have expanded rapidly and much larger settlements, the first real towns, came into existence. By the end of the period, if not earlier, some of these must have been fortified by walls and towers, judging from scenes on a Predynastic slate palette. The Gerzean clay house model (figure 2) represents a sizable structure probably of mud-brick, measuring about 22 by 18 feet (7 by 5.5 metres), with a wooden floor and two small windows set high up in the walls. With the addition of a walled yard or court this simple house has all the essential requisites of a larger multi-roomed Egyptian home. Many of these must have stood in towns like Hierakonpolis, where traces of occupation at this period reached a peak and stretch over an area ¾ mile (1.2 km) across.

The stage was now set for the totally planned urban growth of the Pharaohs.

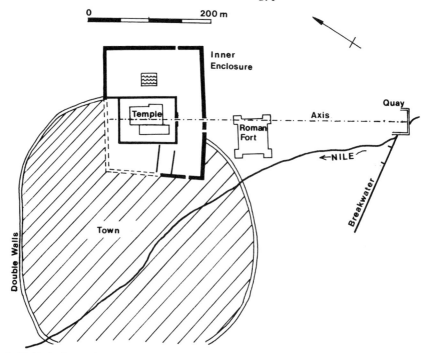

3. Nekheb (El-Kab). Plan of the ancient walled town. (Drawing by Helena Jaeschke.)
4. Nekheb (El-Kab). View of the central area with remains of the temple. (Photograph by Eric P. Uphill.)

3
Provincial or nome capitals

The 36 Egyptian provinces or nomes, later increased to 42 in the New Kingdom, each had its own urban centre which was a combination of local administrative centre and market town. Many, if not all, rose to be great cities in the Pharaonic period and typify the standard naturally growing conurbation. A good example was El-Kab in Upper Egypt, the ancient Nekheb, whose shape exactly reproduced the hieroglyphic determinative for a city (a circle around a diagonal cross), which fully expresses the idea of cross-streets within a walled enclosure of circular or oval shape (figure 3). The shape of El-Kab immediately shows that building was not based on an original rectangular plan but that natural growth had been roughly circumscribed by walls contrived later.

The earliest set of walls found here is double, unlike the much later regular rectangular ones planned on a vast scale. The western part of the town has been partly eroded by the river but the plan by Somers Clarke gives the probable reconstruction of the original layout. In ancient times there were houses in this area, which then measured across its double walls 1279 feet (390 metres) north to south by about 1312 feet (400 metres) east to west. Allowing for the irregular shape, the area within these walls must have been in the region of 25 acres (10 ha). A small section must be deducted for the temple area and central public space (figure 4), but on the ratio used in this study, namely, allowing a maximum of 250 people to the acre (0.4 ha), the town could have had around 6000 people. To safeguard the inhabitants there were two walls, the outer one 9 feet (2.74 metres) thick, the inner one 8 feet (2.44 metres) thick, with a space between of 16 feet (4.88 metres) on average. The total breadth of just over 33 feet (10 metres) may possibly reflect an intended 34 feet (10.5 metres) or 20 Egyptian cubits. The walls were built of crude mud-brick, the inner one standing higher than the outer in places, and were probably built so for defensive reasons.

Two examples will suffice to illustrate the plan and features of the nome capitals, one in the delta and one in the Nile valley. The ancient city of Bubastis, modern Zagazig, in the eastern delta was the home of the cat goddess Bast, an important centre since Old Kingdom times. The mounds and ruins marking the site cover an area of at least 4900 feet (1500 metres) north-south by 1640 feet

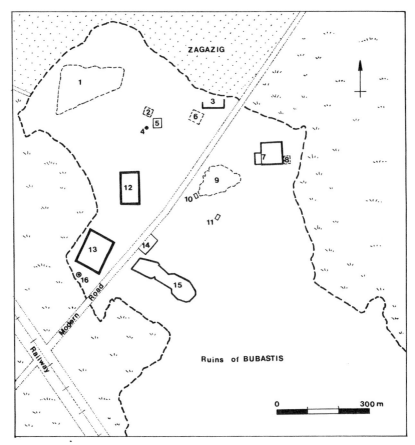

5. Bubastis. Plan of the main building complexes at Tell Basta:1, 2, cemeteries of cats; 3, remains of a palace; 4, Protodynastic tomb; 5, great building; 6, Old Kingdom cemetery; 7, Middle Kingdom palace and enlargement to the west; 8, 9, New Kingdom cemeteries; 10, 11, tombs of Hori; 12, temple of Teti; 13, temple of Pepi; 14, temple of Mihos; 15, site of great temple of Bastet; 16, site of hoards. (Drawing by Helena Jaeschke.)

6. Bubastis. View of fallen granite columns and blocks of the Late Period temple of Bast. (Photograph by Eric P. Uphill.)

(500 metres) east-west or 75 hectares (about 187 acres) and are made up of buildings from the Sixth Dynasty until Roman times (Habachi, *Tell Basta,* page 3, and A. el-Sawi, *Excavations at Tell Basta,* plate 4). To whatever urban nucleus there may originally have been the Old Kingdom Pharaohs added their own walled enclosures containing temples and perhaps dwellings (miniature editions of the royal residences in the capitals). Teti (2340 BC) built an enclosure measuring 350 by 165 feet (108 by 50 metres) with a 13 feet (4 metres) thick girdle wall. Pepi I (2332-2283 BC) built another 280 feet (87.5 metres) north-south by 210 feet (64 metres) east-west with a wall about 16 feet 6 inches (5 metres) thick. It contained a small square mud-brick temple to the goddess. Thus at the end of the Old Kingdom this city, like others, seems to have been composed of a series of royal units added to an existing town centre.

Far more imposing than these modest Sixth Dynasty 'castles' was the great palace complex added under Amenemhat III (1842-1797 BC) in the Twelfth Dynasty. Here the excavated area extends to well over 2½ acres (1 ha), measuring about 377 by 327 feet (115 by 100 metres) not including a cemetery building block

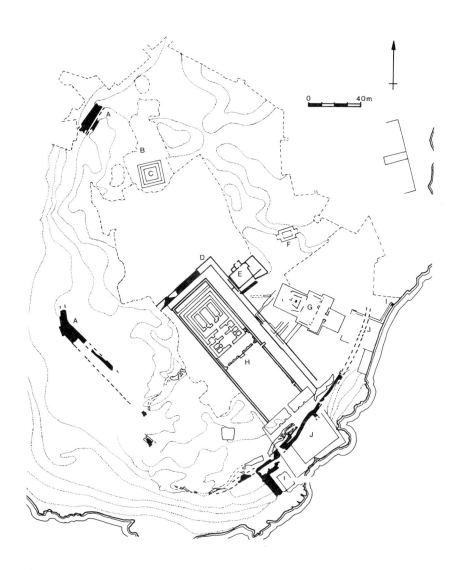

7. Aswan. Plan of the walled town on Elephantine Island: A, town wall; B, necropolis; C, pyramid; D, temple enclosure wall; E, Heqaib complex; F, Amenophis III temple; G, Satet temple; H, Khnum temple; I, Nilometer; J, terrace. (Drawing by Helena Jaeschke.)

to the east. Two courtyards and dozens of halls and rooms make up a massive mud-brick building with underground drainage piping to remove dirty water from tanks in various parts of the layout. The scale can be judged from the dimensions of the main hall, which measured 70 feet (21.5 metres) long by 48 feet (14.8 metres) broad and once had six great wooden columns whose stone bases are about 6 feet 6 inches (2 metres) in diameter. The main entrance faced north due to the north-south alignment of the buildings, a common feature in palaces. A magnificent limestone door lintel found here with a double scene of the king enthroned at his *heb-sed* or jubilee festival suggests the occasion for which the palace may have served or at which it may have been inaugurated. The excavators, however, have seen it as the palace inhabited by the local nomarch or governor. Perhaps it served both functions, being used by the Pharaoh when visiting but serving as the local administrative centre at other times.

A very different type of city was Aswan in the extreme south, on the border of Upper Egypt with Nubia. It owed its importance to two factors, trade with the south, which brought many valuable African products into Egypt, and the granite quarries. There are thus two urban sites, the original on an island, Abu or Elephantine, taking its name from the ivory trade, and Syene on the east bank serving the stone industry. The island formed a natural citadel measuring 1¼ miles (2 km) long by 550 yards (500 metres) at its widest. (Prehistoric remains, pottery and rock carvings show the earliest occupation.) The city's main centre lay at the south end and has been systematically excavated (figure 7). It covered an area of about 4 acres (1.8 ha) in the Old Kingdom and the later area of the walled part or citadel was about 735 feet (225 metres) east to west by at least 665 feet (200 metres) north to south, or 11 acres (4.5 ha), with the city gate in the north-west and the temple of the local ram-headed deity Khnum in the centre. Up to 40 feet (12 metres) of deposits exist here. The Old Kingdom temple covered two-thirds of the walled area, but the Middle Kingdom town was twice as large. Outside the granite (?) walls was an outer city with mainly domestic buildings. Fine houses stood in the south-west temple sector. The nomarchs and great nobles were buried across the river high up in the western bank cliffs, but the funerary shrine of Heqaib exists in the crowded city confines as well as the Graeco-Roman cemetery for the sacred rams near the temple. In the New Kingdom two temples were built by Tuthmosis III (1504-1450 BC) and Amenophis III (1386-1349 BC) but have been destroyed, while a splendid peripheral temple to the goddess Satet, wife of Khnum, and also erected by Tuthmosis III, has been reconstructed. The Khnum temple was rebuilt on a much greater scale in the Thirtieth Dynasty by Nectanebo II (360-342 BC) and added to by Alexander II (317-311 BC).

The other settlement for the quarry workers was under the southern end of the modern town and as such is not accessible, but a small incomplete temple of Isis built by Ptolemy III (246-222/1 BC) and Ptolemy IV (221/2-205 BC) marks the area.

4
Planned settlements:
workmen's villages

Although it is only a small village Deir el-Medina is extremely informative about urban development and is far more interesting than might be expected. There are two reasons for this. First, it is the only area in the vast Theban metropolis to be fully excavated; secondly it was the home of the community of craftsmen and workers in the royal necropolis.

The first village (figure 8) was built there by Tuthmosis I (1524-1518 BC) and this settlement lasted until Tuthmosis IV (1419-1386 BC), roughly one hundred years. It was surrounded by a mud-brick wall, the founder's name being stamped on the bricks. The wall measured about 20 feet (6 to 7 metres) high but was only 3 feet 9 inches (1.15 metres) thick. At this time the central street was built following the line cut out by a torrent in early times and marking the lowest point in the little secluded valley where it was sited. Each end of it was closed by gates at night. The houses were huddled together, saving wall building, and the excavator Bruyère even suggested that a single roof might have covered the whole layout. Such communal life did not submerge the individual, however, and house doors had their owners' names marked on them. The corners of the enclosures were rounded to resist wear and tear. Inside, forty rooms made up the core of the first Eighteenth Dynasty workshops, the village comprising only twenty houses. Even these did not fill the walled area completely and an open space within was probably reserved for animals such as the cattle of the owners. Drinking water formed the most pressing problem for these people, who numbered, say, one hundred in all. It could be obtained only in the Nile valley, a journey of 1¼ miles (2 km). Drilling wells to a depth of 170 feet (52 metres) was an operation quite outside the capabilities of the community. Constant supplies had to be brought by donkey and stored in large storage jars in the houses. A water corvée (requisitioned work) is mentioned on an ostrakon (inscribed potsherd) found here.

As the building operations of the Pharaohs expanded on the west bank at Thebes, so did the little community. Stamp bricks show that the first big increase came under Tuthmosis III, the greatest of the conquerors. The number of workshops increased to 52. The first village had been destroyed by fire, either at this

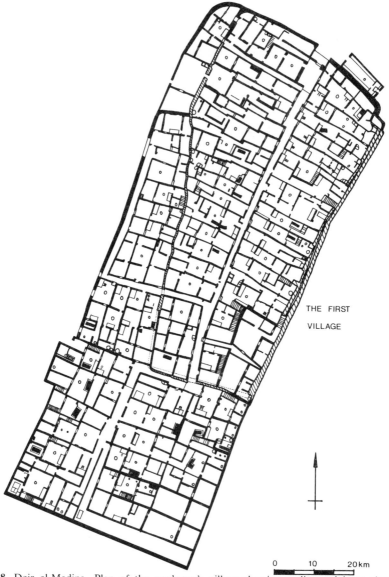

THE FIRST

VILLAGE

0   10   20 km

8. Deir el-Medina. Plan of the workmen's village showing earlier and later phases.
(Drawing by Helena Jaeschke.)

9. Deir el-Medina. View looking towards the western suburbs and tomb area. (Photograph by Eric P. Uphill.)

time or in the Amarna period. Strangely, there was no increase under Amenophis III, the greatest builder at Thebes.

Under Akhenaten (1350-1334 BC) the inhabitants were moved to Amarna to work on the new tombs there and others were perhaps brought from Memphis. Some of the names found at Amarna are similar to those found at Deir el-Medina but it is not certain if these were the same people.

The return to Thebes was marked by certain major changes, the substitution of the family tomb by the individual burial place and a general reorganisation of the village, probably in the reign of Horemheb (1321-1293 BC). The walled village was now expanded to its greatest extent and nine distinct quarters were formed. Streets and ways of access were cut through the blocks of dwellings and funerary concessions (figure 9). The old houses were restored and new ones built, the village being expanded to the south and west to enclose its suburbs, and a new stone wall was built around the whole. Under the Nineteenth and Twentieth Dynasties the community reached its maximum growth. Votive chapels erected in honour of Seti I (1291-1278 BC) show the great prosperity here during his reign. No fewer than 120 families

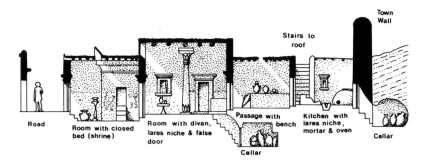

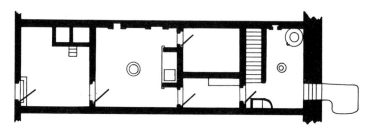

10. Deir el-Medina. Plan and sectional reconstruction of a typical house. (Drawing by Helena Jaeschke.)

worked here, that is to say anything up to six hundred people based on the ratio of five to a home, under the supervision of two chiefs or 'grand masters' assisted by scribes and overseers.

The layout of the village must be understood in order to see living conditions in context. There were now seventy houses within the enclosure and about fifty outside in suburbs to the north and west. The wall was now not so high and thick as that of Tuthmosis and composed only of rough stones set in mud mortar. The reason for this was doubtless the feeling of security and royal control induced by the presence of the Madjoi, a kind of roving police force. The walled area measured 432 feet (131.65 metres) long by 156 to 164 feet (47.5 to 50 metres) wide, a little over 1½ acres (0.65 ha).

An important difference between this village and the earlier one is in the absence of any yards for animals or house courts. Casual planning may be shown by the fact that the house of the Chief of Works, Qaha, is naturally the largest and best in the village, but situated among the poorer houses. There was, again, only one main street but with side alleys, often cul-de-sacs. The community reservoir lay outside the north gate and had to be filled by water carriers from the Nile valley.

Houses were probably first allotted by the government but definitely held on an hereditary basis through the four-hundred-year life of the settlement. Most of them had only one floor and were built to a standard design, those of the first village being built without foundations and with mud-brick walls (figure 10). The later village houses were erected on rubble and had simple walls with stone bases from 6 feet 6 inches to 8 feet (2 to 2.5 metres) high with mud-brick superstructures. They were built in terraces with doors facing each other across the streets, sometimes back to back. They averaged only 17 feet (5 to 6 metres; 10 cubits) wide, but were not regularly spaced out as at Amarna. Wood was used for door posts, lintels, columns and ceiling beams, species including date and dom palm, sycamore, acacia, carob, persea and tamarisk. Rooms were often high, as walls measured from 10 to 17 feet (3 to 5 metres) tall. Roofs averaged 4 to 8 inches (10 to 20 cm) thick. Houses were whitewashed outside

11. Deir el-Medina. View of the front room of a house with 'shrine'. (Photograph by Eric P. Uphill.)

only, the doors being bright red. Inscriptions in red on the jambs and lintels often gave the owners' names. Jambs and columns were of stone in some of the better houses; floors were simply of earth. Basically each house formed the standard ancient oriental tripartite unit with a succession of three rooms of increasing privacy, as well as a passage to a kitchen and rear open area. A typical house would have the following features:

A front reception room (figure 11) opening directly from the street and approached by several steps as it was 16 to 18 inches (40 to 45 cm) below the outside level. A door opposite the entrance led to the main inner living room and a bed-shaped shrine 5 feet 6 inches (1.7 metres) long, 2 feet 8 inches (80 cm) wide and 2 feet 6 inches (75 cm) high dominated one wall. It was approached by steps and may have served the family cult.

A reception room up a step or two from the first chamber and at street level with one or two central columns up to 14 feet (4.3 metres) high. It invariably had a family divan 8 inches (20 cm) high and with a low wall 2 feet to 2 feet 4 inches (60 to 70 cm) high at each end. Against another wall were a small altar and offering table and slotted niches for the household deities in the form of busts (compare the Lares and Penates of the Romans).

A small cellar often placed under the second reception room, approached by a flight of steps and covered by a wooden trapdoor.

A small room (or twin rooms) opening off the main room and serving as a bedroom cubicle or private workroom for the household women. A passage with a bench led to the rear.

A kitchen and service area with a large domed bread oven, kneading trough and water storage facility, with perhaps another family shrine niche.

A staircase to the flat roof, where the family could sit or store things.

A rear cellar for food storage or a rectangular grain silo.

Windows were, as normally, set high up in the walls with stone or wooden grilles.

5
Lesser royal residences and frontier towns

Kahun has often been called a mortuary priests' town or, even more improbably, a workmen's settlement since its discovery and hasty excavation by W. M. F. Petrie in 1889-90, but it was the pyramid city and probably the royal residence of Sesostris II (1897-1878 BC), situated near the entrance to the channel that took Nile waters to the Fayum province, and was called *Ha-Senusret-hotep* or 'The House Sesostris is satisfied.' It centred around the massive valley temple of the pyramid which was situated about ¾ mile (1.2 km) to the west. The temple stood on high rocky ground and was approached by a sloping ascent built of large stone blocks, dominating the city. Papyri as well as archaeological evidence show that the settlement was fully inhabited only during the builder's reign, afterwards having a small population living among many abandoned buildings.

The plan (figure 12) is divided into two very unequal parts. That to the west, with its walls measuring about 340 feet (104 metres; 200 cubits?) east to west by 1125 feet (350 metres) north to south, to the temple wall, or around 8½ acres (3.5 ha) in extent, was reserved for what appear to have been workmen's houses and humbler dwellings. The eastern quarter, also walled, was nearly three times as large, being about 940 feet (287 metres; 550 cubits?) east to west by apparently the same distance north to south, although only 800 feet (244 metres) of this was cleared. The total area would thus have amounted to approximately 24 acres (9.5 ha), and with the other quarter and temple area included nearly 35 acres, about 1148 by 1345 feet (350 by 410 metres, 14 ha) in all. If there was a balancing urban area south of the temple and its approach then the city would be nearly double the size. This may be compared with the city attached to the sun temple of Niuserre at Abu Gurob (about 2500 BC), which measured 984 feet (300 metres) north to south. From the plan the city walls appear to have measured about 10 feet (3 metres) thick at the base and would (as free-standing ones) have been about 20 feet (6 metres) high. They were not of the fortified type and lacked towers or strongly defended gates. The eastern sector had many different sizes of houses.

In the western quarter the regular rectangular or grid street plan with evenly spaced house blocks is at once apparent. The

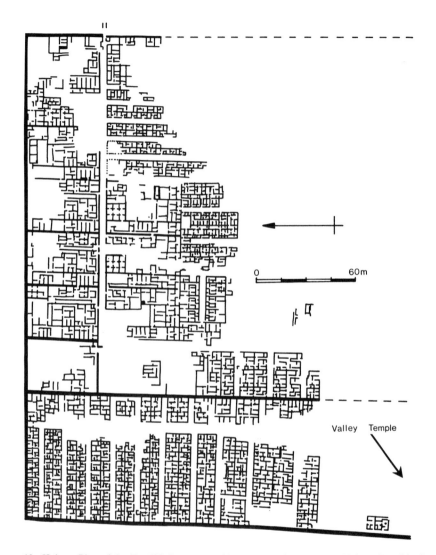

12. Kahun. Plan of the Twelfth Dynasty residence town. (Drawing by Helena Jaeschke.)

Egyptian architects had evolved the street and avenue plan two thousand years before Hippodamus! Blocks of buildings in rows averaging about 150 feet (46 metres) long branch off from the west wall and run towards longer and wider blocks which begin at the north wall and cross the eastern part. Petrie noted how easily a single night-watchman could guard the whole area. Eleven parallel streets 13 feet (4 metres; 8 cubits) wide ran east-west from a main north-south road 26 to 30 feet (8 to 9 metres) broad, ample widths in an age before wheeled transport, when the donkey was the main beast of burden.

Drainage was not neglected and all the streets appear to have had a stone channel running down the middle to remove surplus or dirty water from cleaning houses and the street. Baked brick tiles formed the paving, which sloped down to the central drain.

All the house units here followed a basic design pattern, rooms being grouped together in sets of six with only one outer door to the street. The architect used round units throughout: 10, 5, 4, 3, and 2 cubits. The smallest dwellings simply had a little open court with two rear rooms opening from each other, while at the side was a larger room with a staircase leading to the flat roof (figure 13). Smaller rooms were tiny, only 6 to 7 feet (2 metres) wide, the larger 13 by 7 feet (4 by 2 metres). A superior workman's house had larger and more numerous rooms, while still larger houses with varied designs sometimes had a doorkeeper's office beside the entrance, with a passage to a central court or light well, and may thus have been for officials. The largest type of house found was for overseers: it had a passage leading to a court with three rooms opening from it and a door to an inner court with two further rooms. These courts were probably half roofed over for shade. Some rooms were roofed with brick barrel vaults, thus saving on valuable timber beams and columns, but wooden roofing with reed thatching covered by a layer of mud was more normal. Doorways were arched and measured about 42 inches (1.05 metres; 2 cubits) wide. No traces of upper floors were found but the considerable number of staircases might imply partial first floors of a room or two in some cases, as later at Amarna. Stairs went up in two flights and averaged 25 to 28 inches wide (63 to 71 cm). House plans were so regular that when Petrie drew three from a single row, superimposed, differences of hardly more than an inch or two (2.5 to 5 cm) appeared except on the wall of the north side. These houses contained from five or six to twelve or more rooms and passages.

Outside walls were, as usual, plain white plastered; inside some had paintings as well as dados, in red, yellow and white, showing household scenes such as jars on stands or the occupants. Columns were octagonal with slightly tapering bases 20 to 24 inches (50-60 cm) across the bottom, their centres placed at 3 or 4 cubit (about 6-8 foot; 2 metre) distances. The shafts were about 10 inches (25 cm) in diameter. In many chambers conical-shaped granaries were found, measuring 5 feet 6 inches to 6 feet (1.75 metres) in diameter. Doors had wooden frames, bolts and thresholds, with stone sockets for the pivots.

The buildings of the eastern quarter were divided into eight basically different types by Petrie. For most purposes these may be reduced to six types classified as: the so-called acropolis and adjacent guard building to its south, together with six other similar mansions along the north wall and three more to the south of a great east-west road in the north sector; the houses built against the inner wall dividing this quarter from the western; the storerooms behind the great southern mansions; the workmen's street behind the great southern houses; five similar streets of workmen's houses on the east of the city; some further undesignated buildings at the extreme east side of the city.

The house on the raised rock platform at the north-west of this quarter, which Petrie called 'the Palace', is no larger than those alongside it and is so placed simply to allow for the natural topography of the site, which also causes a slight jog in the town wall at this point. Each of these ten great houses exceeds any of those at Amarna in scale and complexity, not excluding the vizier's, and one might hazard a guess that they were intended for royal princes rather than nobility. They measured 138 feet wide (42 metres; 80 cubits) by 198 feet long (60 metres), thus covering over half an acre (0.2 ha), and contain around seventy large courts, rooms and passages on the ground floor alone. Even assuming that they were entirely single-storeyed, the number of inhabitants in each must have been very great, one alone covering an area equal to fifty of the smallest workmen's houses or fifteen of the medium-sized dwellings. The only entrance was from a single door surmounted by a stone lintel representing a rolled-up mat covering. Passages led to three different quarters basically representing the offices and business parts, the servants' quarters, and the private family rooms. Most spectacular of the apartments were: the *mandara* or court 63 by 37 feet (19 by 11 metres) with nine columns along the south side; a west atrium-type court 32 feet (10 metres) square with a central sunk stone water tank ringed by twelve palm columns; the main living hall of about 25

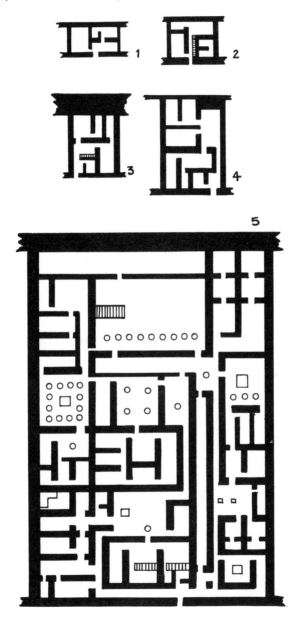

13. Kahun. Comparative plans of houses, from workmen's (1) to a mansion (5). (Drawing by Helena Jaeschke.)

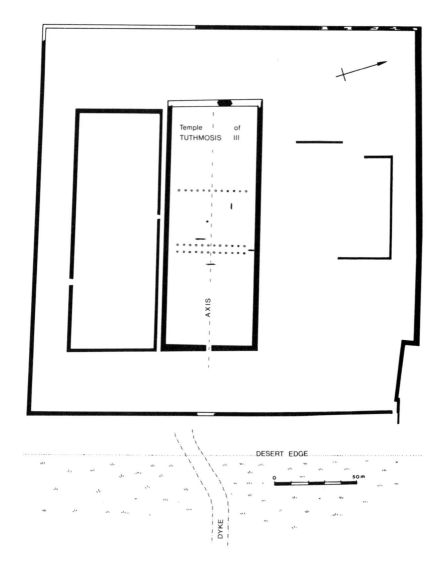

14. Gurob. Plan of the Tuthmosis residence enclosure. (Drawing by Helena Jaeschke.)

feet (8 metres) square with four columns like an Amarna mansion; and the master's bedroom with a bed alcove and presumably a wind-chute for cooling it.

Such was the city of Kahun in which Petrie stated he found 2145 rooms, claiming he had cleared about three-quarters of the city, whose total rooms he put at over 2700. In fact he had cleared only half to two-thirds and his figure of three hundred smaller houses, ten or twenty larger and ten great mansions needs to be raised by more than he allowed.

Allotting an average of five people as the minimum for the smaller houses and a maximum of ten for the larger, with up to one hundred for the mansions and their dependencies, the following figures are obtained: 1500 + 200 + 1000 or 2700 people in all for the area Petrie cleared. This gives figures of 4050 or 5400 for the whole urban area if it covered the area suggested above, agreeing well with an estimate of 5000 people by Badawy, *Egyptian Architecture,* volume II. He does not give the figures on which this estimate was based but presumably assumed a certain density allocation for a given area. This could represent a minimum, given the ratio of 250 people per acre, which on a postulated house area of 32 acres (13 ha) out of 35 acres (14 ha) total city area would indicate a total of 8000 people. This must be the maximum on the present evidence, but more people may have lived in the smaller and medium-sized houses, which would more than offset a somewhat smaller number in the mansions.

Gurob is a very different town which was dug by Petrie in 1889-90. A later season in 1920 added more information on the site, which lies just south of the entrance to the Fayum at the other end, from Kahun, of a large regulator dyke. The original name is as yet unknown but it was built by Tuthmosis III (1504-1450 BC) and lasted until the reign of Merneptah (1212-1202 BC), when it became ruined, but still retained some slight occupation as late as Ramesses III (1183-1151 BC). The presence of Aegean pottery here in the time of Amenophis III suggests not only foreign trade but that this was a royal residence. Despite damage done to the temple inscriptions by Akhenaten, his mother Queen Tiye seems to have visited the town in this period, if she did not actually live there.

The main urban area (figure 14) is formed by an enclosure measuring about 776 feet (238 metres) wide by 760 feet (233 metres) deep, a little over 13½ acres (5.5 ha). But these measurements taken across the walls must allow for the fact that they are of variable thickness on the plan, owing, no doubt to

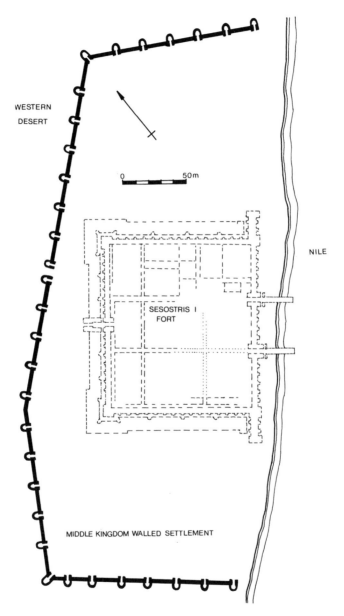

WESTERN
DESERT

0   50m

NILE

SESOSTRIS I
FORT

MIDDLE KINGDOM WALLED SETTLEMENT

15. Buhen. Plan of the outer walled area of the Middle Kingdom settlement. (Drawing by Helena Jaeschke.)

their very ruinous state. Inside were two main enclosures and a lesser one, the central one within its brick wall being that of the temple 100 cubits broad (171 feet; 52.3 metres). That alongside is not so clear but was possibly a royal palace, all these walls being 10 feet (3 metres) or more thick. Remains of other walls to the right of the temple may have been for storerooms or even a sacred lake, but another small temple was also situated here. The rest of the enclosure, if not parts of that described, must have been occupied by houses, but without any plans it is unwise to speculate on their form or the possible population.

Evidence of metalworking and commodities used by craftsmen indicate the functions of some of these inhabitants. Towns such as these could have been built as frontier post settlements and their layout copied throughout the whole Egyptian empire. Two examples from Nubia and Kush show what they were like in the Middle and New Kingdoms.

Buhen's first Middle Kingdom enclosure (figure 15) may have preceded the building of the inner earlier fortress erected during the joint rule of Amenemhat I (1991-1962 BC) and his son Sesostris I (1971-1928 BC). Its purpose was arguable. W. B. Emery, who discovered it, believed it was erected for protection while the fortress was built, an explanation also advanced by J. Vercoutter for the extra-mural settlement at the comparable site of Mirgissa. Equally, at both these sites and others in Nubia, there must have been trading posts and local communities who needed defence as well as the garrisons in the royal forts. The town, if such it was, was thus distinct from the military settlement although it was planned, having a brick wall 2335 feet (712 metres) long enclosing an area about 1380 feet (420 metres) north to south by 490 feet (150 metres) east to west, as measured across the walls. The layout thus covered 15 acres (6.3 ha), less the area of the inner fort after that was built, 564 by 525 feet (172 by 160 metres). The town wall was fairly substantial, being 13 feet (4 metres) thick, and strengthened by 32 open rounded bastions projecting 21 feet (6.5 metres) but with their walls only 7 feet (2.15 metres) thick. As later there was one gate in the middle of the west side, the positions of any others were not established; indeed the wall itself is missing on the river bank. It has been calculated that to defend these walls with three men per bastion and six more on each 72 foot (22 metre) interval between them 276 men would be required, or, on a two and four men ratio, 184. This does not allow for the river side. Taking wives and children into consideration, and there would have been other non-military inhabitants, a population of from 1500-2000 seems to be a minimum estimate: based on acreage estimates, even allowing for the inner fort, the higher figure seems likely. Several Middle Kingdom houses and administrative buildings existed alongside the north moat of the inner fort, but these probably date from the time of the second outer enclosure wall system built during the time of Sesostris III (1878-1841 BC) when the whole area was virtually turned into a fortress. It is not possible to be certain of the functions of the outer enclosure because it is too denuded, but serpentine walls dating probably to the first enclosure period may be compared to similar ones at Mirgissa, where Vercoutter found central rectangular blocks of brick buildings were surrounded by these walls against which stone huts were built for individual soldiers' families. A strong internal east-west wall may therefore have divided off such a camp area from the bigger houses and administrative blocks. At Mirgissa the lower town had a great enclosure area whose brick wall ran for over 1650 feet (500 metres) north of the hilltop fortress. The outer settlement here may well have been a trading post also.

Sesebi (figure 16) was a new town built by Akhenaten at the beginning of his reign between the Second and Third Cataracts. Its walls form a rectangle 885 feet by 655 feet (270 by 200 metres), 13 acres (5.4 ha). They were 15 feet (4.6 metres) thick and still stood 13 to 16 feet (4 to 5 metres) high at the time A. M. Blackman excavated the site in 1936-7. They were also strengthened at regular intervals by massive buttresses 10 feet (3.15 metres; 6 cubits) wide and projecting 8 feet 6 inches (2.65 metres). Four gates, one in each wall, gave access to the interior. They were paved with stone, doubtless to allow wheeled vehicles through, and had a drainage channel beneath the paving. The north-west quarter was entirely taken up by a large tripartite temple with a spacious forecourt 158 feet by 103 feet (48.2 by 31.5 metres), originally dedicated to the Theban Triad by the king when he still called himself Amenophis IV. The rest of the northern quarter was too denuded to form any idea of its original use, but this could have also been reserved for official buildings rather than housing.

It is the slightly smaller southern quarter which contained the dwellings of the inhabitants. These were disposed in an ordered street system and were constructed with rather thin walls. As they had been continually altered throughout the town's existence their planning was confusing but there was once again a regular street grid for the tightly packed homes, which had no grounds

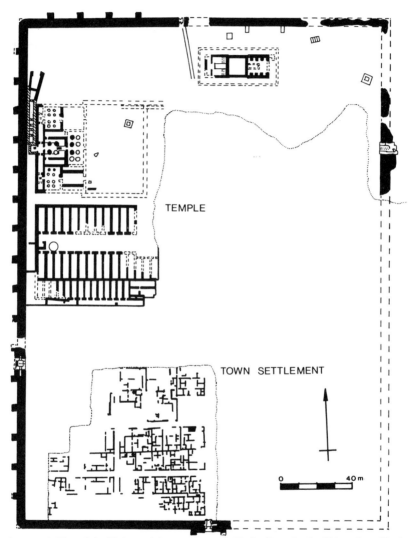

TEMPLE

TOWN SETTLEMENT

0   40 m

16. Sesebi. Plan of the Eighteenth Dynasty town in Kush. (Drawing by Helena Jaeschke.)

owing to lack of space and were often built back to back. The excavators deduced upper floors from stairs and fallen column bases of first-floor rooms. Many cellars were provided, while the whole area was separated by a wide street from the town wall as customary in military installations. A rough count suggests up to 24 houses could have been built in a 164 foot (50 metre) square (about ⅔ acre), or, less certainly, sixteen larger ones, with from eight to twelve such squares available according to whether the north quarter alone, or the eastern half of the central zone also, was used for official buildings. This gives totals of 192 or 128 and 288 or 192 houses. Allowing five people to a smaller, or eight people to a larger, house, the total inhabitants would have been 960 or 1024, 1140 or 1536. The population may thus have been in the order of 1000 to 1500, which, on a ratio of about 180 to the acre (0.4 ha), is well within the 250 limit.

The *Hwt W'rt* administrative cities were another type of settlement established by king Sesostris III to establish firmer and more direct government control over Egypt. There were several of these, the most famous being the northern one, later enlarged to form the capital of the Hyksos invaders in the seventeenth century BC and known to history as Avaris, while another possibly existed under Amenemhat III at Hawara. The name means 'House of the Messengers', derived from the fact that they served as bases for the royal runners. Avaris is almost certainly represented by the Middle Kingdom site of Khata'na, centred on the great 60 acre (24 ha) mound of Tell Dab'a, and at its peak covered 500 acres (202 ha), double the site of Qatna in Syria, the largest Hyksos period Asiatic town defended by a mighty earth rampart. In a sense Khata'na represents the growth of many urban settlements from at least as early as the First Intermediate Period until the beginning of the New Kingdom, but the Sesostris town, like the monuments of his predecessor Amenemhat I here, must have been a formidable planned foundation, with a triangular harbour covering about 100 acres (40 ha) set beside it in a low depression.

6
Towns for funerary priests

The Pharaohs even established urban communities to serve their needs for the hereafter, settlements to last for ever rather like an enormous extension of the medieval chantry chapel endowments, whereby the priests of their *Ka* (essential spirit) could offer food in their mortuary temples. One such town at Giza has been fully excavated, that of the Fourth Dynasty queen Khentkawes, the whole complex being cleared by Selim Hassan in 1932-3.

It was first built at the end of the Fourth Dynasty and apparently flourished until the break-up of the Old Kingdom at the end of the Sixth Dynasty, after which it was abandoned and soon covered with sand. The southern and western parts were certainly never re-occupied. It was small compared with the city of Kahun. Only fifteen houses were excavated and the area covered was relatively small.

The main walled area was L-shaped (figure 17). The total length of the northern arm, measured from the tomb on the west to the eastern boundary wall, was 485 feet (148 metres), its average width far less than that of the eastern arm, which was only about 138 feet (42 metres; 80 cubits) as measured across the town walls. Part of the plan is missing because the area has been buried by modern cemeteries and houses, but assuming a rectangular shape for this section also, the total area of the town would be only around 1½ acres (0.65 ha). Other buildings outside may belong to the adjacent town of king Menkaure (2532-2504 BC), attached to his valley temple.

The thick enclosure wall may have been intended to measure 8 feet 6 inches (2.6 metres; 5 cubits) thick at the base and around 17 feet (5 metres) high originally, thus completely screening the one-storeyed houses for maximum privacy. The plan shows that the entire layout was designed to specific requirements: straight streets, regular intersecting byways and housing groups each with their own granaries and reservoirs.

It is not possible to say whether the houses had more than one storey as the walls are too denuded to indicate window arrangements, but the absence of staircases suggests only one floor. The mud-brick walls were coated with a hard yellow plaster 1¼ inches (3-4 cm) thick. Chemical analysis showed it contained the following elements: common salt (sodium chloride), gypsum (hydrated calcium sulphate), powdered limestone (calcium carbonate), coarse sand and small quartz grains, fine silica and

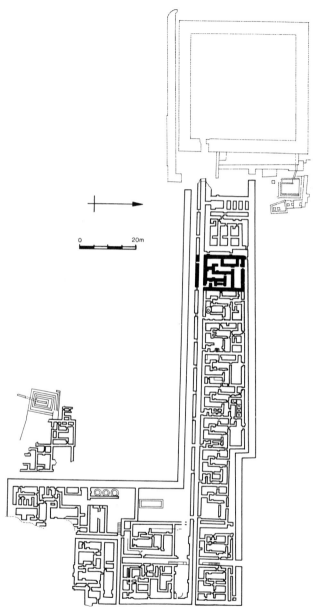

17. Giza. Plan of the funerary town of Queen Khentkawes. The solid outline denotes the position of the house shown in figure 19. (Drawing by Helena Jaeschke.)

aluminium with iron oxides. Tests indicated that it was the silica and the salts which made this plaster capable of withstanding the climate, including rain, for over 4500 years.

The houses may be divided into three classes by size and grouping: mansions in the south-east section near the Menkaure valley temple; larger houses in the western sector near the queen's tomb; smaller houses in the north-east section reached by a subway under the causeway leading to the tomb.

Starting from the north-west sector nearest the tomb, the room to the south (number 1), opening on to the street, was possibly a guard chamber or for temple officials. Then comes the first of a row of houses, the largest here measuring about 56 feet east-west by 49 feet north-south (17 by 15 metres). It should be noted that, like all the other houses in this row, there are two entrance doors, one from the south street and one into the northern passage by the wall. There were also gate openings in the southern street wall giving access to the wide freeway running east to west and also serving the eastern arm of the town. The south street itself has a gate opening at the east end and this gives direct access to the tomb area which could have remained open and been used when the two quarters of the town were closed for the night.

The next six houses were identical, measuring roughly 38 by 49 feet (11 by 15 metres), and had these features in common (figure 19): a porter's lodge (23), reception room (27), living room (24), two communicating bedrooms (21 and 22), an open court (26) giving access to a kitchen (25), water storage room (29) and domestic offices (30). The plan takes into account climatic features, the kitchen being placed south-east of the living rooms so that the prevailing north wind would carry away cooking smells. Many ovens found by the excavators in the kitchens still contain the ashes of the last fires lit in them. The fifth house had the reception room space occupied by a granary with five circular grain bins.

The four smallest houses lay beyond these, measuring about 46 by 34 feet (14 by 10.5 metres). A limestone gate threshold with door sockets was found here in the north wall, and a surprisingly modern feature in the form of a subway giving access to the southern houses of the east section without going outside the walls or across the causeway after the gates were shut. It was approached by twelve rock-cut steps on the north and a ramp on the south, being roofed with large limestone slabs. Another east-west street from the valley was linked by four steps to the courtyard which had grain bins in its eastern arm. Alongside this

18. Giza. View of the Fourth Dynasty houses in the town of Khentkawes, looking west. (Photograph by Eric P. Uphill.)

to the north was a massive water tank or reservoir 95 feet by 27 feet (29 by 8 metres). The mansion in the south-west corner of the town may have belonged to the official in charge of the granaries and storerooms; a large recess found in the east wall of room number 182 is deep enough for a seat and contained a dais. Another mansion with twelve rooms (numbers 152-63) measured 73 by 49 feet (22.5 by 15 metres) and contained remains of mural decoration.

If twelve people are allowed for the west house, ten each for the row of six, eight for the smaller houses at the end of the north quarter and up to twenty for each of the five mansions in the east sector, a total of two hundred people is reached for the town, considerably below the maximum density suggested of 250 to the acre.

Papyrus Harris (which details the king's gifts to the Egyptian temples) shows that Ramesses III gave 160 towns in Egypt and nine more in Syria and Kush to his great religious endowment. Besides being dedicated to the principal gods of Egypt, these also served the royal funerary cult on a scale as yet unequalled in history. Most of the 113,433 workers and their families probably lived in them and many, if not all, of these settlements may have been built or rebuilt by the king.

Medinet Habu, the King's Theban funerary temple, occupied

first place among these with not only 62,626 workers to support it, but also priests and officials who lived within the outer fortified walls of the temple enclosure. As this outer sector had many features in common with such sites as Tell el-Retabeh in the Wadi Tumilat, where Ramesses built a great fortified enclosure with a massive wall for the town, it can serve to illustrate what these foundations were like.

The inner walled enclosure, built first, was the official quarter and contained the temple, a small palace, storerooms and administrative offices of the funerary establishment (figure 20), and covered about 6 acres (2.5 ha). The outer enclosure round it, 16¾ acres (6.5 ha) in all, was defended by a brick wall more than

19. Giza. Isometric reconstruction of a typical house in Khentkawes. (Drawing by Helena Jaeschke.)

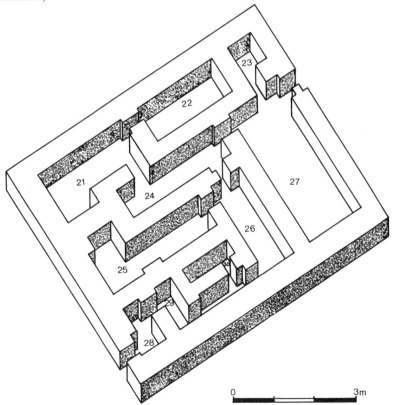

0   3m

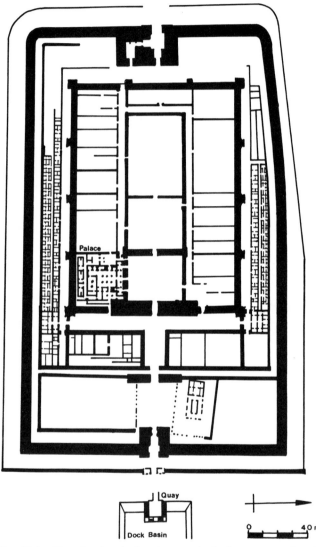

20. Medinet Habu. Plan showing the housing zone in the funerary complex of Ramesses III. (Drawing by Helena Jaeschke.)

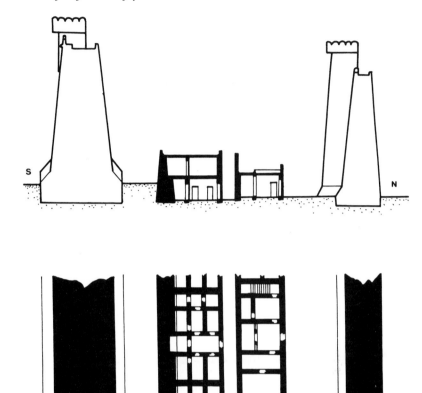

21. Medinet Habu. Plan and section of two typical houses. (Drawing by Helena Jaeschke.)

50 feet (about 16 metres) high and 34 feet (10.5 metres; 20 cubits) thick at the base, with an outer rampart and wall set over a ditch. Two more 'aerial' palaces or pavilions occupied the upper floors of the great east and west gate towers.

The town lay between the inner enclosure wall and a low girdle wall that ran inside a raised walk resembling a Roman pomoerium (free way for the rapid movement of troops) at the foot of the main outer wall. It was a compact and entirely self-contained urban entity like that of Khentkawes. As the area nowhere measured more than about 72 feet (22 metres) wide, including the street and the alley that served the dwellings, the

architect had to make the houses long and narrow to fit in the
maximum number. Their entrances were set in the longer sides
facing inwards towards the inner enclosure, one row served by
blind alleys that communicated only at the ends with entry areas
and exits, and which measured 5 feet (1.5 metres) wide compared
with the 20 feet (6 metres) of the roads. Each housing block was
thus completely cut off from the other and self-contained. The
considerable differences in design also suggest alternative functions or that two different classes of people lived in the two zones.
The approach route from the fortified area to the outer houses
possibly indicates their use by guards or temple patrols, assuming
they were not simply stores, while those within, looking towards
the temple, would seem to be connected with priests and temple
officials. One resident here a little later, in the reign of Ramesses
XI (1098-1070 BC), was the scribe Butehamun from Deir
el-Medina village, who moved in here for safety and lived in a
house with a four-columned and a two-columned room. The
houses themselves were substantial (figure 21). Those in the inner
zone measured about 53 by 21 feet (16 by 6.5 metres) and had a
central entrance hall or court with a roof at the back supported by
two octagonal columns. Six more side rooms and a staircase
leading to either a first floor or a flat roof completed the design.
The outer zone houses, measuring 35 by 21 feet (10.7 by 6.5
metres), were very different and consisted of an entrance hall
leading to a rear room with up to nine cell-like side rooms, all of
which could have been brick vaulted. These again may have had a
first floor.

7
Imperial cities

Capitals

One fundamental question is which city did the ancient Egyptians consider to be their chief city and metropolis? Here two factors should be understood: firstly, climate and politics meant that Egypt needed two administrative centres for the Two Lands, Upper and Lower Egypt; secondly, these centres would vary from age to age. In ancient monarchies the administration would be where the king was, the royal residence city, but this does not necessarily equate with the capital in the modern sense of the word. As regards the New Kingdom the question can be resolved by reference to two epithets that Pharaohs added to their names, 'Ruler of Heliopolis' and 'Ruler of Thebes', which must indicate where the seats of power were considered to be. A third candidate for a capital, particularly in the Old Kingdom, must be Memphis, 'The Balance of the Two Lands', and those cities used before or after these periods may have been either capitals serving short-term needs or else royal residences.

Classification is also difficult. In general these metropolis cities were natural growths over many centuries, but all of them show intensive royal planning and rebuilding, as would be expected in a capital more than anywhere else, hence they must be included in the second category of urban settlements.

Heliopolis, Egyptian Iunu, was undoubtedly the largest city in New Kingdom Egypt. Its mound area covered 9 square miles (23 sq km) in the early twentieth century, while its metropolitan area extended 26 miles (41 km) from Tell el-Yahudiyeh in the north to a port on the Nile at what is now Old Cairo. Ideally situated for growth on a trade route out of Egypt, it was the centre of learning and, in addition to having the chief sun temple of Egypt, was famous for its astronomical school. Remains of buildings on the temple site go back to the Third Dynasty, but it seems certain that there was a major community here long before that time. Today the few visible remains are at the site of the temple of Re Atum, the creator god, but much of the stonework and other material has been carried off for buildings in other cities as far afield as Alexandria. Nevertheless some idea of its size can be gained from the fact that the Late Period double walls round the temple site extend 3400 feet east to west by 2900 feet north to south (1050 metres by 900 metres), enclosing 220 acres (89 ha) as compared

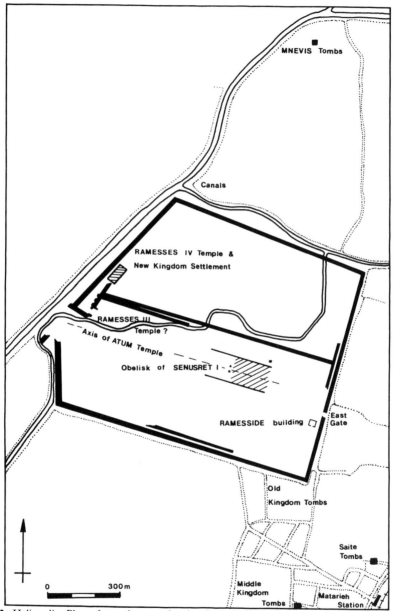

22. Heliopolis. Plan of temple area showing Late Period walls and principal features. (Drawing by Helena Jaeschke.)

23. Heliopolis. View of the walls and general area of the Ramesses temple. (Photograph by Eric P. Uphill.)

with Karnak's main 60 acre (24 ha) enclosure. This is sub-divided into two nearly equal parts, the southern being centred on the obelisk of Sesostris I, today raised some metres above its original position (figure 22).

Petrie's so-called Hyksos camp is almost certainly the remains of a New Kingdom enclosure wall system, possibly a parallel to Ramesses III's at Yahudiyeh, and recently a gate of this king has been found at the western part of the site. Brick buildings of Ramesses II (1279-1212 BC) and Ramesses IV (1151-1145 BC) as well as houses and isolated stone blocks attest to the fact that every major ruler of the New Kingdom, as well as earlier monarchs, erected monuments here (figure 23). Much more excavation will be needed to give any adequate picture of this most important site.

Memphis is more rewarding, although still a very fragmented site compared with Luxor. The tradition recounted by Herodotus, that Menes, the first Pharaoh (about 3050 BC), diverted the Nile towards the east side of the valley in order to build the city on reclaimed land or else over a natural mound, may have some truth in it as research has shown that the earlier part does stand on higher ground to the west of the site. This does not mean that the settlement was unique as many other towns in the Nile valley

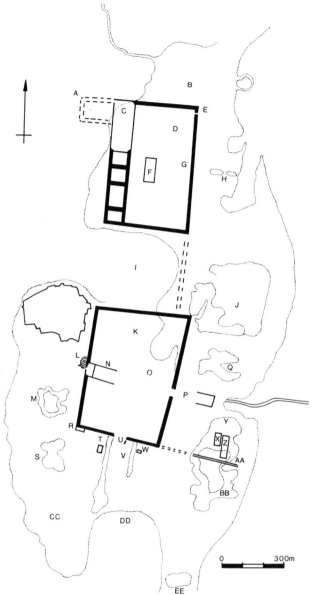

24. Memphis. Plan of the central city area and principal monuments: A, extension to C; B, temple of Neith (?); C, palace of Apries; D, late enclosure; E, great gate; F, small temple; G, Kom el-Kelb; H, Kom daf Baby; I, lake of Ptah; J, Kom en Naby; K, Kom el-Khanzir; L, pond; M, Kom el-Fakry; N, west hall; O, temple of Ptah; P, Ptolemy IV approach; Q, Kom el-Abbayn; R, temple of Ramesses II; S, Kom er Rabya; T, Hathor temple; U, Colossus; V, Dromos; W, temple of Ramesses II; X, temple of Merneptah; Y, Kom el-Qal'a; Z, palace of Merneptah; AA, late wall; BB, Kom el-Qalama; CC, Siamen; DD, Temple of Apis (?); EE, Kom Helul. (Drawing by Helena Jaeschke.)

25. Memphis. View of the site of the Ptah temple showing ruins of the great hall. (Photograph by Eric P. Uphill.)

and the delta were similarly placed. It may be that later Egyptians remembered Memphis best among all the other urban founda- tions of the early dynasties who undertook the gigantic task of controlling the inundation and river by constructing huge dykes and water basins. Advantageously placed at the point where the Nile divided into several branches, the early town soon grew fast, partly because of the foundation of pyramid towns like that of Pepi I (2332-2283 BC), from which it took its name Men-nefer, 'Enduring and beautiful'. These settlements seem to have coalesced over the ages until by the Roman period, when the town still prospered, the city centre as shown by its remains stretched 1¾ miles (2.8 km) north to south, although it was rather narrow east to west (figure 24). This certainly did not include the whole inhabited area, whose suburbs must have stretched far beyond. Hence Diodorus, the first-century Greek historian, makes its circuit 150 stadia or between 17 and 18 miles (28 km), but it is not clear what he included. He certainly did not include the enormous necropolis area, the pyramid fields which, stretch- ing for miles from north to south, form the greatest cemetery ever known.

The official quarter centres on two great enclosures each of about 60 acres (24 ha) with its mud-brick walls, the palace of king Apries (589-570 BC) of the Twenty-sixth Dynasty to the north, and the Ptah temple (figure 25) south of it. The temple has yielded the most archaeological evidence to date, a huge hypostyle hall of Ramesses II with at least four lesser temples to the south dating to the same reign.

More relevant to the present study is the palace of his successor, Merneptah, which was discovered to the south-west of the main temple. Discovered at a depth from 16 to 18 feet (5 metres) below modern ground level, it forms the eastern wing of an obviously large building complex contained within a massive girdle wall. The hieratic nature of the monarch's office is well illustrated by the almost cult-like layout of the buildings, recalling the planning of a temple in its rigid orientation with axis due north and sequence of courts and halls. A northern gatehouse with an upper hall, possibly containing a window for the king's appearances, led to a spacious court surrounded by 34 limestone columns and measuring 175 feet long by 80 feet wide (53.5 by 24.5 metres). A tremendous doorway 20 feet (6 metres) wide and about 23 feet (7 metres) high led into the first reception hall 80 feet (24.5 metres) broad and with twelve columns larger than those of the court. These like all the other stone fittings of the palace were richly ornamented, their inscriptions inlaid in faience and the figures carved in relief on the shafts overlaid with thick gold leaf. The throne hall beyond was, if possible, even more magnificent, 60 feet long by 41 feet wide (18 by 13 metres) with six columns and a throne dais 13 feet 6 inches by 16 feet 6 inches square (4.2 by 5 metres), on which panels showed bound captive figures representing the world's races, negro, Libyan, Sherden (sea peoples) and so on. Golden winged discs symbolising the god Horus were set over the doors leading to the private rooms at the rear and sides, among which were the king's ceremonial bedroom and bathroom. Such a dwelling gives an indication of what has been lost at Memphis and hope that future excavation will reveal more.

Thebes, the southern capital, the Waset of the Egyptians, began its long history as a simple nome or provincial capital, but under the Middle Kingdom Pharaohs grew to rival the northern metropolises. It again demonstrates the fact that apparent haphazard growth is often the result of planned quarters, or else the re-planning of pre-existing ones by later kings. Diodorus makes its circuit 140 stadia, or about 16 miles (25.5 km), which

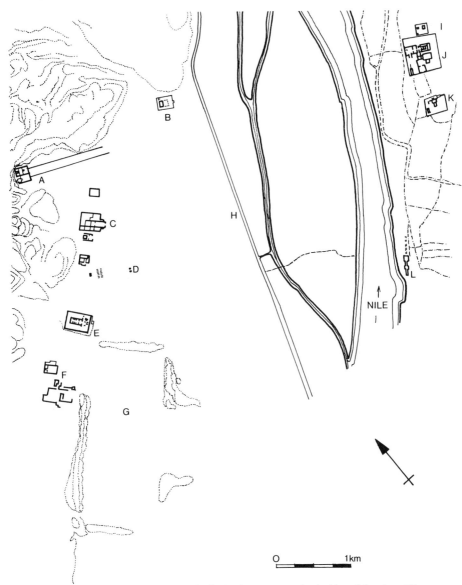

26. Thebes. General plan showing principal urban areas on both sides of the river. West bank: A, Deir el-Bahri; B, Qurna temple; C, Ramesseum; D, colossi of Memnon; E, Medinet Habu; F, Tehen Aten complex; G, harbour; H, canal. East bank: I, Temple of Monthu; J, Karnak, Temple of Amun; K, Temple of Mut; L, Luxor temple. (Drawing by Helena Jaeschke.)

must thus include all the west bank settlements and temples as well as the eastern city, a perfectly correct description as texts of the New Kingdom refer to mayors of the east and west parts. The 16 square miles indicated do not include the cemeteries but do comprise an area with not only gardens but also fields adjoining the river. A truer total of inhabited land would seem to be about 1970 acres (about 796 ha) at maximum comprising about 950 acres (384 ha) on the east bank and 1020 acres (412 ha) on the west. When it is remembered that a modern computation puts the area of Karnak temples and their associated buildings at 1⅕ square miles (3 square kilometres), this estimate may be seen as a modest one.

Looking from the first pylon at Karnak a line-up with the temple of Hatshepsut at Deir el-Bahri (figure 26) appears immediately significant, because it is next to the Eleventh Dynasty temple of King Mentuhotep (2060-2010 BC). This Pharaoh reunited Egypt after a long period of division and used his new great resources to create a splendid new capital, the first known major city to be laid out on axial lines in ancient times. Previously kings had done this for pyramid complexes with a causeway connecting the valley temple to the upper part of the complex, but here is a scheme stretching for 3 miles (5 km) across the valley and Nile itself. Starting from the king's tomb in the western mountain, it aligns with central Karnak, where remains of the period have been found. A causeway ¾ mile (1.2 km) long descended from the court of the temple to reach a valley entrance building, where there may have been a priests' town and canal to the river. On the plan of Thebes a line drawn continuing the causeway ends up in the Karnak area, where the royal residence must surely have been. The Twelfth Dynasty kings, although ruling from the north, maintained a major administrative centre here and huge halls and other buildings have been found at the rear of the sacred lake at Karnak.

Tuthmosis I built a palace and temple at Karnak and every Pharaoh until the end of the Twentieth Dynasty seems to have added something here as well as constructing a funerary complex on the opposite bank.

Amenophis III seems to have tried to integrate all the many temples and quarters of the city and thereby form a coherent whole like Mentuhotep's scheme, but on a much vaster scale. He laid out an avenue that led to the temple of Mut, which he rebuilt, while another avenue of jackals representing Anubis led to his vast funerary temple on the west bank. The scheme was later

TEHEN ATEN PALACE COMPLEX

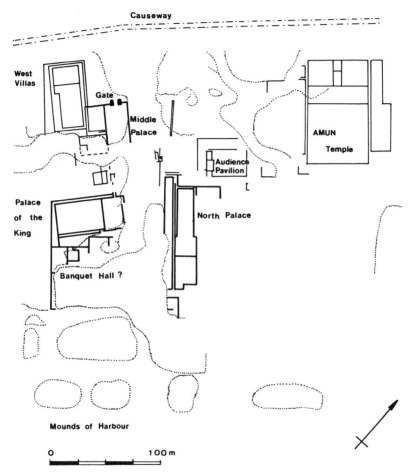

27. Thebes. General plan of the Malkata palace complex of Amenophis III. (Drawing by Helena Jaeschke.)

vastly extended by Nectanebo I (380-362 BC), who built a causeway avenue 1½ miles (2.5 km) long from the temple of Luxor to Karnak, flanked the whole way by sphinxes.

Pharaonic residences

The purpose of the residence city erected by Amenophis III to the south of his gigantic funerary temple on the west bank at

28. Thebes. View of the mounds of Birket Habu, the artificial harbour of Amenophis III. (Photograph by Eric P. Uphill.)

29. Thebes. View of the remains of the Malkata palace looking north. (Photograph by Eric P. Uphill.)

Thebes was, from the evidence of jar sealings found at the site, to serve as a setting for his three magnificent *sed*-festivals or jubilees, when representatives came from the entire known world to take part as guests. Its name appears to have been Tehen Aten, 'Splendour of the Aten', an epithet shared by the king and also by the royal barque used at a festival inaugurating Queen Tiye's pleasure lake.

The main palace complex (figure 27), as far as excavated, covers about 80 acres (32 ha) and remains the largest and most representative of Egyptian royal dwellings, its general name Per Hai, 'House of Rejoicing', foretelling the central city complex at Amarna. To serve the city's needs a colossal harbour now known as Birket Habu was excavated (figure 28). Its mounds, still 50 feet (15 metres) high, mark an area 1⅝ miles (2.6 km) long by ⅝ mile (1 km) wide with an extension on the east where the Nile waters could enter. Some impression of its size may be gained from the fact that about 385,000,000 cubic feet (11,000,000 cubic metres) of material was piled up, making it equal in bulk to more than four Great Pyramids on a site equal to the Assyrian city Nimrud or 900 acres (360 ha).

The Per Hai or Malkata falls into two sectors orientated in general on a north-south axis, and although labyrinthine it shows a very carefully considered, ordered plan. The northern sector was mainly reserved for official buildings, while the southern had domestic ones such as private palaces, stores and houses (figure 29). An intricate corridor system connected up all the major sections, of which six main divisions can easily be traced from north to south: the temple of Amun, the royal chapel built mainly of brick but covering, with its huge court, an area equal to the contemporary principal stone temple at Karnak; the audience pavilion with its associated buildings, which is the centre of the whole design, being physically placed in the middle; the harem and servants' quarters (wrongly termed the North Palace by the excavators), which screen the private palace of Amenophis from the public parts of the palace; the west villas and large houses for officials on the south-west of the site; the middle palace, suggested as being for the use of the crown prince Akhenaten; the 'Ah palace or private quarters of the king, with alongside it the so-called Palace of Tiye, probably in reality a banqueting hall complex.

Each of these sectors is as large as any normal royal palace in the ancient east and clearly shows its function. Stables, chariot houses and craftsmen's quarters must also be included in the complex as a whole.

The temple served for the important religious ceremonies of the main three days of the festival, while the audience chamber contained a platformed building with a window for the king to appear at when interviewing visitors in the court below. Like many other buildings on the site, this was adorned with faience tiles, in blue and other colours, and gilded plaster. The harem buildings contained a whole series of small tripartite houses 42 to 46 feet by 23 feet (13 to 14 metres by 7 metres) square for attendants, generous in scale compared with the 18 feet wide (5 to 6 metres) Deir el-Medina houses. In addition there were several larger suites of rooms, one of which, with eleven great rooms, measured about 130 by 100 feet (40 by 31 metres) and has been identified as that of a royal princess such as Sitamun.

Most interesting of all is the king's private palace, a monolithic unit without courts measuring, as far as it has been excavated, about 425 to 440 feet (130 to 135 metres) north to south by 180 feet (55 metres) east to west. Within are a whole series of columned halls once with magnificent wall paintings and throne daises, the central one being about 90 by 37 feet (27.5 by 11.5 metres) and having two rows of eight columns. Opening from it at either side were four sets of queens' and princesses' apartments and at the southern end an inner hall with the king's bedroom and bathroom.

Akhenaten chose a magnificent site for his new residence city and religious centre in middle Egypt at Akhetaten, 'the Horizon of the Aten' (modern Amarna), or rather, as he himself stated in the boundary stelae inscriptions marking the metropolitan limits, 'the god chose it for himself'. Here was unlimited building space on a wide crescent-shaped plain running 6 miles or so (10 km) north to south by up to 3½ miles (5 km) east to west. Only a narrow strip of cultivation existed by the river, but on the opposite bank lay a great fertile plain 12 miles (20 km) across before the desert on the west side was reached. This could form the farmland for the city, a royal garden estate, and was included in the geometrically precise tract of land delineated by the fourteen great rock-cut boundary markers. The total city area within these was in the region of 112 square miles (290 sq km). The urban area proper was a ribbon development along the east bank of the Nile, broken in places by the wadis which run across the site but in general continuous from a guard building blocking the narrow pass at the north end to what may be a similar one at the south. An estimate has placed the built-up area at 1100 acres

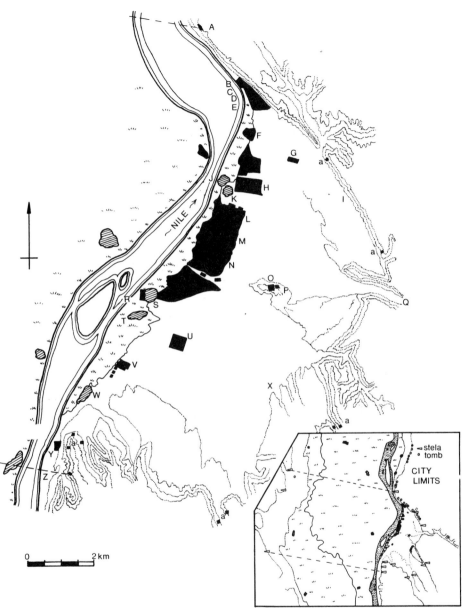

30. Amarna. General plan of the area of Akhetaten and of the city boundaries: A, north city limits; B, customs house; C, great wall; D, east palace; E, north city; F, north palace; G, altars; H, north suburbs; I, northern tombs; J, El Till; K, Esbi; L, great temple area; M, palace; N, main city; O, tomb chapels; P, workmen's village; Q, royal wadi; R, river temple; S, Hagg Qandil; T, El Amarea; U, royal enclosure; V, Maru Aten; W, Hawata; X, southern tombs; Y, southern entrance; Z, south city limits, (a) stelae. Inset: Lines of city territory. (Drawing by Helena Jaeschke.)

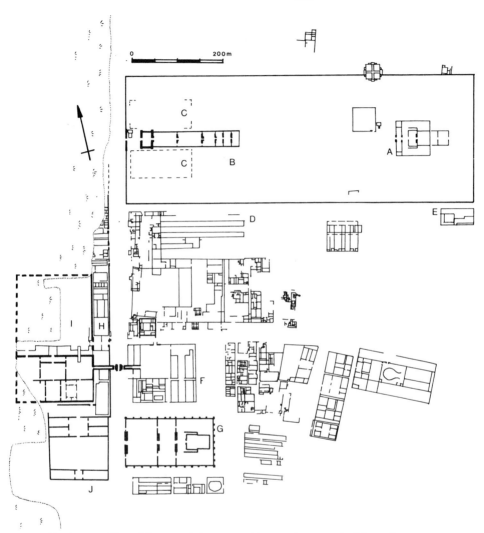

31. Amarna. Plan of the central city zone and its most important buildings: A, sanctuary; B, Gem Aten; C, offering tables; D, stores; E, High Priest's house; F, private palace; G, *Hwt* Aten temple; H, harem; I, major temple complex; J, coronation hall. (Drawing by Helena Jaeschke.)

(440 ha) but this does not include parts not yet excavated, and a figure of 3000 acres (1200 ha) may be more realistic. The immense scale is best conveyed by the fact that Rome within the walls of Aurelian covered nearly 3500 acres (1400 ha).

The official buildings and central city area were the only parts laid out on a truly regular plan. The rest of the urban land appears to have been built up in piecemeal sections, great nobles' houses gathering those of their dependents round them. Nevertheless there was some general ordered arrangement and three great roads ran from north to south with streets opening off them. The eastern highway was named by its German excavators High-priest Street; at times it attained a width of more than 170 feet (50 metres; 100 cubits) but like the other roads here had no paving. Parallel to it at approximately 525 feet (160 metres; 300 cubits) lay a less imposing thoroughfare, Street A, but further west again lay a magnificent road, the modern Sikhet es-Sultan or 'King's Road', which served the royal palaces and temples and was about 130 feet (40 metres; 75 cubits?) wide, in the central city area (figure 31). The grid pattern was to some extent masked by cul-de-sac streets that ended in the middle of the islands of houses thus formed.

The king himself had no fewer than five palaces ranging from the great northern one to the royal villa alongside the smaller of the two Aten temples (figure 32). Four temples to the god were found in the central area and innumerable shrines and houses and other buildings existed throughout the city. There were also

32. Amarna. View of the harem court in the central palace looking north. (Photograph by Eric P. Uphill.)

workshops, police headquarters and a foreign office, with records, where the famous letters were stored.

An analysis of housing conditions took a sample of more than five hundred houses excavated in the central city, based on Borchardt's excavations of 1911-14, and was able to distinguish eight types of dwelling, belonging to three classes of inhabitants. The lowest group, forming 54-59 per cent of the population, lived in four of these types in which the crowded conditions were evident, whereas the middle class, forming 34-37 per cent, inhabited three other types of house whose features indicated a comfortable living standard. The upper classes formed 7-9 per cent of the population and lived in spacious houses or mansions with ample areas round them for several yards with workshops, stables, granaries and even gardens, and often had several small houses attached for servants.

Typical of these mansions was the house of the Vizier Nakht, the house itself measuring 85 feet (26 metres; 50 cubits) square, with a porch projecting 30 feet (9 metres) at one corner, and containing thirty rooms on the ground floor alone. This again had the usual tripartite division, the northern third including a 40 foot (12 metre) long loggia reserved for public functions, the central area round the great hall for semi-public living and the rear for the owner's private life with his family. A middle class house tended to be simply a smaller version of this.

Per Ramesses, literally 'House of Ramesses', the delta residence of Ramesses II, was the last and perhaps greatest of these imperial residence cities (figure 33). What Akhenaten could not complete in fifteen years could be accomplished on a more massive scale in the long reign of Ramesses, and further additions were made to it after his death until its abandonment after two centuries. So vast was the layout that the old centre of Seth worship at Khata'na (figure 34), which had a shadowy but continuing existence after the expulsion of the Hyksos, was rebuilt as the southern of the four new city quarters. The other three were named after the local goddess of Nebesheh (north), Astarte (east) and Amun (west), while the centre which contained the royal palace was termed Bekhen or castle. While suburbs containing merchants, ordinary Egyptians and foreign residents must have stretched for miles along the banks of the eastern branch of the Nile, the government and religious buildings were located in a natural stronghold defended by the river, canals and sand saddle promontories which covered approximately 4 square miles (10 sq km).

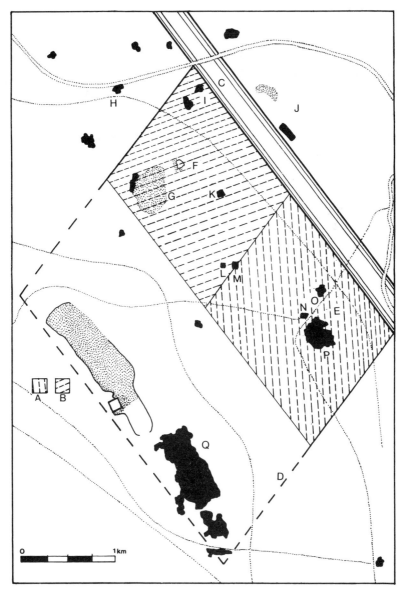

33. Per Ramesses. Plan of the main city area with the location of Avaris and the southern sector defined: A, certainly established area of Per Ramesses; B, Avaris; C, Pelusiac branch of the Nile; D, probable extent of the city; E, a palace of Ramesses; F, harbour; G, Tell Dab'a; H, Khata'na; I, Ezbet Helmy; J, Ezbet Rushdi el-Kebira; K, Ezbet Rushdi el-Saghira; L, Ezbet Kosti; M, Ezbet Yani; N, Kafr Silmi; O, Ezbet el-Ysergi; P, Qantir; Q, Es-Sama'na. (Drawing by Helena Jaeschke.)

34. Khata'na. View of Tell Dab'a mound looking north across the harbour. (Photograph by Eric P. Uphill.)
35. Qantir. View of the site of the palace of Ramesses II looking south. (Photograph by Eric P. Uphill.)

The palaces and royal workshops are known to cover an area of 22 acres (9 ha) but may well extend further (figure 35). Temples to all the principal deities of Egypt existed in the central city while the metropolitan shrine of Amun-Re may have rivalled Karnak and possessed an enormous pylon and gateways with four colossal statues of the king, two seated and two standing. Many of the state ministries were here, vast granaries, storage depots and, above all, the core of the army and troops used in the king's wars.

Court poets wrote eulogies on the splendours of the palace, halls and balconies and, if they are to be believed, the faience decoration beggared description: the archaeological remains, now mostly under fertile fields, indicate that it was of unparalleled richness. Walls as well as floors, columns and doorways were encrusted with innumerable varieties of tilework in the form of captive figures with inlaid robes, river and garden scenes, heraldic devices and rosettes. The throne daises were especially magnificent with steps depicting prostrate captive figures representing the Nine Bows, or races of the world, for the king's feet to tread on when he mounted, flanked by balustrades with large figures of lions 2 feet 4 inches (70 cm) high, biting captives. Such richness has never been surpassed, if rarely equalled, in history, and forms a fitting note on which to end this survey of ancient Egyptian urban life.

8
Town and city sizes

Deir el-Medina	1½ acres (0.65 ha)	Khata'na	494 acres (200 ha)
Khentkawes	1½ acres (0.65 ha)	Memphis	1136½ acres (460 ha)
Buhen	8¾ acres (3.55 ha)	Amarna	1087 to 2965 acres
Medinet Habu	10 acres (4 ha)		(440-1200 ha)
Elephantine	11 acres (4.5 ha)	Thebes (east bank)	840 acres (340 ha)
Sesebi	13¼ acres (5.4 ha)	(west bank)	988 acres (400 ha)
Gurob	13½ acres (5.5 ha)	(total)	1828 acres (740 ha)
El-Kab	24½ acres (10 ha)	Per Ramesses	2471 acres (1000 ha)
Kahun	34½ acres (14 ha)	Heliopolis	5683 acres (2300 ha)
Bubastis	185¼ acres (75 ha)		

9
Nome capitals

Egyptian name	Greek form	Modern site
UPPER EGYPT		
1 Abu)	Elephantine)	Island
Sunu)	Syene)	Aswan
2 Djeba	Apollinopolis	Edfu
3 Nekhen	Hierakonpolis	Kom el-Ahmar
4 Waset	Thebes	Luxor
	(Diospolis Magna)	
5 Gebtiu	Koptos	Quft
6 Iunyt	Tentyris	Dendera
7 Hut	Diospolis Parva	Hu
8 Abdu	Abydos	El Araba-el-Madfuna
9 Ipu	Panopolis	Akhmim
10 Tchebti	Aphroditopolis	Ifteh
11 Shashotep	Hypselis	Shutb
12 Per Anty	Antaeopolis	Qua el-Kebir
13 Saut	Lycopolis	Asyut
14 Kis	Cusae	El-Qusia
15 Khemnu	Hermopolis	El-Ashmunein
16 Hebnu (Later)	Theodosiopolis	Area Zawiyet el-Maiytin
17 Kasa	Cynopolis	El-Queis
18 Hut Benu	Hipponos	El-Hiba
19 Spat Meru?	Oxyrhynchus	El Behnesa
20 Ehen Insi	Herakleopolis Magna	Ehnasiya
21 Shemen Hor?	Nilopolis	Area Abusir el-Melek
22 Per Idet?	Aphroditopolis	Atfih

Egyptian name	Greek form	Modern site
LOWER EGYPT		
1 Men-nefer	Memphis	Mit Rahina
(earlier Inbu Hedj)		
2 Sekhem	Letopolis	Ausim
3 Per Nebet Imau	Gynaecopolis	Kom el-Hisn?
4 Tcheka	Prosopis	Menuf?
5 Sai	Sais	Sa el-Hagar
6 Khaset	Xois	Tell Sakha
7 Per Hut Neb Imenti	Metelis	Macil near El-Atf?
8 Per Atum	Heroonpolis	Tell el-Maskhuta
9 Dedu	Busiris	Abusir Bana
10 Hut Ta Heri Ib	Athribis	Benha
11 Hesebt	Pharbaethos	Horbeit area
12 Tchebnetcher	Sebennytos	Samannud
13 Iunu	Heliopolis	El-Matariya
14 Djani	Tanis	San el-Hagar
15 Per Djehuti	Hermopolis Parva	Damanhur
16 Per Banebded	Mendes	Tell el-Ruba
17 Behdet	Diospolis Inferior	Tell el-Balamun
18 Per Bastet	Bubastis	Tell Basta
19 Per Wadjit	Buto	Kom el-Farain
20 Per Sopdu	Arabia	Saft el-Henna

(There is still some doubt about the locations of capitals with a question mark.)

36. (Opposite) Map of Egypt showing the location of sites mentioned in the text.

10
Bibliography

General

Badawy, A. *Egyptian Architecture,* I-III. I, Giza 1954; II and III, Berkley and Los Angeles 1966, 1968.

Davies, N. de G. 'The Town House in Ancient Egypt', *Metropolitan Museum Studies* 1 (1929), 233-55.

Fairman, H. W. 'Town Planning in Pharaonic Egypt', *Town Planning Review* 20 (1949).

Lampl, P. *Cities and Planning in the Ancient Near East.* Studio Vista, London. Egypt is covered on pages 23-32.

Smith, W. Stevenson. *The Art and Architecture of Ancient Egypt.* Second edition revised by W. Kelly Simpson, Penguin, 1981.

Ucko, P. J., Tringham, R., and Dimbleby, G. W. *Man, Settlement and Urbanism.* Duckworth, 1972. A very complete general study on all aspects of urbanism. Section Two subsection A deals exclusively with the Nile valley.

Specialist

Bietak, M. *Avaris and Piramesse. Mortimer Wheeler Archaeological Lecture 1979.* Proceedings of the British Academy, Oxford University Press, volume 165, 1981.

Brunton, G., and Engelbach, R. *Gurob.* British School of Archaeology in Egypt, volume 41, 1927.

Emery, W. B., Smith, H. S., Millard, A., et al. *The Fortress of Buhen. The Archaeological Report.* The Egypt Exploration Society, Oxford University Press, 1979.

Frankfort, H., and Pendlebury, J. D. S. *The City of Akhenaten,* part II. Egypt Exploration Society, Oxford University Press, 1933.

Hayes, W. C. *Most Ancient Egypt.* Chicago University Press, 1965.

Hassan, Selim. *Excavations at Giza,* volume IV, 1932-3. Cairo, 1943.

Hoffman, M. A., and others. *The Predynastic of Hierakonpolis.* Egyptian Studies Association Publication number 1. Cairo University Herbarium, 1982.

Jeffreys, D. G. *The Survey of Memphis I.* Egypt Exploration Society, 1985.

Nims, C. *Thebes of the Pharaohs.* Elek, 1965.

Peet, T. E., and Woolley, C. L. *The City of Akhenaten,* part I.

Egypt Exploration Society, Oxford University Press, 1923.

Pendlebury, J. D. S., et al. *The City of Akhenaten,* part III (two volumes). Egypt Exploration Society, Oxford University Press, 1951.

Petrie, W. M. F. *Kahun, Gurob, Hawara.* Kegan Paul, Trench and Trubner, 1890.

Petrie, W. M. F. *Illahun, Kahun and Gurob, 1889-90.* Nutt, London, 1891.

Spencer, A. J. *Brick Architecture in Ancient Egypt.* Aris and Phillips, 1979.

Thomas, A. P. *Gurob: A New Kingdom Town,* I and II. Aris and Phillips, 1981.

Uphill, E. P. *The Temples of Per Ramesses.* Aris and Phillips, 1984.

Index

Page numbers in italic refer to illustrations

FOI
APR 17 2024